Water Made Wine

Water Made Wine

A parish team approach
to marriage preparation

MARGARET GRIMER

Foreword by Jack Dominian

Darton, Longman and Todd
London

First published in 1986 by
Darton, Longman and Todd Ltd
89 Lillie Road, London SW6 1UD

© 1986 Margaret Grimer

ISBN 0 232 51680 4

British Library Cataloguing in Publication Data

Grimer, Margaret
    Water made wine: a parish team approach
to marriage preparation.
    1. Marriage—Religious aspects—
Christianity
    I. Title
    261.8′3581   HQ734

    ISBN 0–232–51680–4

Phototypeset by Input Typesetting Ltd, London SW19 8DR
Printed and bound by Anchor Brendon Ltd,
Tiptree, Essex

Contents

For those clergy and laity who work together in parish marriage teams and so accept a shared responsibility for couples marrying among them.

Foreword

Two events have recently focussed attention on marriage. The first was the statement on this sacrament by the Second Vatican Council. After centuries, during which the emphasis was entirely legal, the Council emphasized the personal and loving qualities of marriage and, indeed, called it a 'community of love'. Thus a whole new chapter of the theology of marriage has started.

The second phenomenon has been the monumental increase in divorce in the last twenty-five years in the whole of western society. Such an attack on the fundamental Christian belief of the permanency of marriage has needed a response on the part of the Christian community. This response has been practical and it has involved both a better preparation for marriage and a much greater support for the married after the wedding.

Margaret Grimer's outstanding little book is concerned with preparation for marriage, which has now become a necessary step for all couples undertaking this vocation. Although thoroughly practical, the book is embedded in the post-Vatican II philosophy of marriage, and so in one step those undertaking marriage and their counsellors will be undertaking a journey into contemporary theological thinking.

The book is written in simple, concise and precise language, and spells out clearly how parishes can assemble a team of trainers in the work of marriage preparation. Every parish (or when necessary more than one parish can combine) should avail itself of the opportunity to carry out this essential work, and this book will prove invaluable in the enterprise.

JACK DOMINIAN

Acknowledgements

My thanks are offered
to all the parish marriage teams whose training I have shared and from whom I have learned so much;

to Willie and Priscilla Dean and to Gwen and John McCormack, who work as parish marriage volunteers and who helped make the text useful for couples in training;

to Mgr Vincent Nichols and to Fr Chris Fallon who helped me to think more deeply about the key role of the clergy in marriage preparation;

to Rev. Peter Chambers, Adviser on Marriage to the House of Bishops and to Joy Thompson, experienced and enthusiastic animator of parish marriage teams, for reading the text through Anglican eyes and assuring me of its value to members of the Church of England;

to Rev. Mary Frost for giving me a Free Church perspective: to Mary I apologize for the text's assumption that the Christian minister is invariably male;

to my co-workers in the Catholic Marriage Advisory Council and especially to my inspiring colleague, Fr Anthony Ford. Anthony has shared so much of my experience in training parish marriage teams that it is now difficult to know which ideas are his and which my own. I pay tribute to his vision, but for what is written in the following pages I take full responsibility.

MARGARET GRIMER

Cana

There was a wedding at Cana in Galilee. The mother of Jesus was there, and Jesus and his disciples had also been invited. When they ran out of wine, since the wine provided for the wedding was all finished, the mother of Jesus said to him, 'They have no wine.' Jesus said, 'Woman, why turn to me? My hour has not come yet.' His mother said to the servants, 'Do whatever he tells you.' There were six stone water jars standing there, meant for the ablutions that are customary among the Jews: each could hold twenty or thirty gallons. Jesus said to the servants 'Fill the jars with water,' and they filled them to the brim. 'Draw some out now', he told them, 'and take it to the steward.' They did this; the steward tasted the water, and it had turned into wine. Having no idea where it came from – only the servants who had drawn the water knew – the steward called the bridegroom and said, 'People generally serve the best wine first, and keep the cheaper sort till the guests have had plenty to drink; but you have kept the best wine till now.'

This was the first of the signs given by Jesus: it was given at Cana in Galilee. He let his glory be seen, and his disciples believed in him.

(John 2:1–11)

1

Taking Steps

'We want to get married. Can you fix it for us?'

Two people, often two strangers to the man opening the door, stand on the doorstep of presbytery, vicarage, clergy house or manse.

The first contact is being made in a relationship whose aim is for the clergyman to greet the couple again at the altar steps of his church and to celebrate with them, their families and friends the union of their life and love.

What is the role of the clergy in the progress of the couple from doorstep to altar step? Is the part they play central and indispensable? How much time and effort will it involve? How can this be made most effective? Can the laity be mobilized to take their share in the responsibility of preparing this couple for their wedding?

'Come in. Tell me about yourselves.' As the couple cross their threshold the clergy know they are accepting a key role. It is to the clergy that couples initially come. It is the clergy who offer the first welcome, make the first contact, show the first interest in this couple's story and in the journey that has led them to make their request to marry in this place and in this Christian Church.

Each of the clergy has the indispensable role of being the named person responsible to church authority for conducting a wedding which their particular church will recognize. Few people enjoy doing paperwork, and most couples are entirely oblivious of the diligent effort involved in smoothing a couple's path through the bureaucratic requirements of the Christian

Church as an institution. Yet many couples set some value on their marriage being recognized in the eyes of their Church. It is thanks to the clergy if the technicalities are conducted so tactfully that they are a reassurance rather than a misery. It is the clergy, too, who must check out whether the attitudes and intention of the couple asking to marry are compatible with their Church's understanding of Christian marriage. Are they celebrating the same thing? More exactly, are they celebrating enough of the same thing to be able honestly to share the same words and actions to express what this marriage can mean?

Do the couple intend to be faithful to each other? Do they mean their marriage to last until death? Is their attitude one of openness to new life? Checking out such questions is all the more difficult where clergy with minds full of churchy terminology meet couples with heads apparently full of such matters as wedding cars, receptions, dresses, bridesmaids, flowers and videos. It is a tribute to the professional skill of the clergy that sufficient agreement is usually reached about the meaning of marriage for the wedding plans to proceed and for a date to be fixed.

It is the clergy, secondly, who stand on behalf of the parish community and of the Christian Church to receive the vows of the couple as they pledge their life and love. It is they who ask, 'Are you ready to love and honour each other as man and wife for the rest of your lives?', and who bless the couple in the name of Christ and his Church.

To extend a welcome, to conduct a valid marriage, to ensure that the couple understand the meaning which marriage can have for Christians, to receive the vows of bride and groom and to bless them in the name of Christ and his Church, these are the clergy's traditional roles. Often taken for granted, they are central and indispensable for every Christian wedding.

But today's clergy are also finding themselves in totally new roles. Priests are seeking practical ways of exercising a new kind of priestly leadership, one that fosters among the laity a sense of co-responsibility for the life and mission of Christ's church. Many take their cue from the statements about the

2

laity in *Lumen Gentium*, one of the documents of the Second Vatican Council:

> Those faithful are by baptism made one body with Christ and are established among the People of God. They are in their own way made sharers in the priestly, prophetic and kingly functions of Christ . . . they are called in a special way to make the Church present and operative in these places and circumstances where only through them can she become the salt of the earth. Thus all lay people, by virtue of the very gift bestowed upon them, are at the same time witnesses and living instruments of the mission of the Church herself 'according to the measure of Christ's bestowal' (Eph. 4:7).

In the progress of an engaged couple from doorstep to altar step, today's clergy find themselves asking: What is the role of the parish community? How are the laity enabled to share in this couple's welcome? If they are to find the honest water of their love for each other somehow changed into the precious and gladsome wine of a Christian marriage, what part can married lay Christians play in bringing this about? When on their wedding day groom and bride walk through the congregation to stand before Christ's ordained minister, will this symbolize any help they have received from the laity towards their preparation for their marriage? How are the clergy, especially the celibate clergy, to make the enlivening and exciting but new and radical shift which places trust in the married laity and mobilizes, animates and encourages them to play their full part in a parish's marriage preparation scheme?

This book advocates the formation of parish marriage preparation teams. They consist of several married couples, under the leadership of the parish clergy, who together take responsibility for the quality of preparation offered to couples marrying in the parish church. Much of the book is devoted to the motivation, aims, selection and training of these parish couples, and to the details of the sessions which they can offer to couples about to marry. Clergy who foster and support such a parish marriage team are actively working to develop co-responsi-

3

bility, helping to 'build up the church' and creating a joint ministry of clergy and laity at the service of those about to marry.

In the story which is often read at weddings, it was Jesus who quietly orchestrated the miracle of Cana. He gave simple instructions: to fill pots with water; to pour it out; to bring it to the steward. The steward did not know the source of the wine he tasted, neither did the guests, nor the bride and groom. But the servants knew.

The priest who invites and encourages parish couples to form a marriage team may seem to take a back seat for some of the wedding preparation. That he initiated it may go unnoticed. Yet, when the couple stand before him to make their promises, the parish team will recognize that it was their priest exercising a new kind of vision and leadership, who enabled them to form an effective team and to prepare this couple well for their marriage.

In such parishes it may be a member of the clergy who first opens the door to a couple asking to marry. The couple is soon aware that he represents a whole community.

2

The Couple on the Doorstep

'We've come to arrange a wedding'.

In one year 344,000 couples in England and Wales reached a stage in their relationship when they felt confident enough to say, 'We are committed to each other. We belong together. And we are ready to declare this to the world at large and especially to our friends and relations and those who are dear to us.' For 177,000 of these couples it was not enough to state their commitment before a civil registrar; they came to a Christian community and asked God's people in that place to witness their promises and to celebrate with them their life and their love.

This book is written from within the Christian Church and addresses the Christian communities these 177,000 couples approach. It asks us, clergy and laity, the whole people of God, to look at what the couple are requesting when they come to arrange a wedding with us. What do they want? What do they need? It asks us to look at how we respond. Do we give them what they ask for? Do we meet their needs? Do we give them the best we have to offer? Is there a better way for the local church to serve the men and women who ask to marry among us?

CHRISTIAN UNEASE ABOUT MARRIAGE TODAY

Congratulations. That's wonderful! Even as we say it, we feel uneasy, fighting down the questions. One out of three

5

marriages ends in divorce – will theirs be one of them? The outlook for couples marrying in Christian churches is not very different from the others – are we in any way responsible for this? How do we feel about hearing over the years the procession of couples making lifelong vows in our local church and learning later that, long before death, the divorce court has separated so many of them? How do we feel about the survivors, so often finding their marriage enslaving when it could be liberating, a small death when it might be life-enhancing, a wasteland without understanding when it 'ought' to be a community of life and love? And, faced by this couple on the church doorstep, the most immediate question of all: as well as helping them to arrange their wedding, can we also prepare this couple better for their marriage?

DO COUPLES WANT MARRIAGE PREPARATION?

What are the couple saying? 'We've come to arrange a wedding.' They're not sick, they have not come with problems they can't handle, their relationship is in good enough order for them to want to declare it publicly. If they came only to buy a wedding, so to speak, what right have we to sell them marriage preparation? Because it's good for them? For a generation past in Roman Catholic churches very competent marriage preparation courses have been run by counsellors of the Catholic Marriage Advisory Council. Many couples arranging to marry in a Catholic church are given the option of attending. About 10 per cent do so, and the overwhelming majority of those express their satisfaction. What about the other 90 per cent? Maybe they feel that they are the best judges of what is good for them, and that marriage preparation courses are not what they want or need. Is there something else the local church can offer them?

In recent years in Roman Catholic churches it is gradually becoming accepted that all sacraments are prepared for very thoroughly within the parish community. First communion, confirmation, baptism for your new baby, the Christian initiation of adults – the word has got about: if you ask for a sacrament, expect a lengthy and thorough preparation. Expect the parish community to share the preparation – parents, catechists, people of faith – just as they will share in the celebration. So it might be thought simple within the Roman Catholic tradition, where marriage is considered one of the seven main sacraments marking the milestones of Christian life, to insist upon similar, parish-involved preparation.

Yet as a sacrament marriage is unique. Other sacraments are asked for singly, by people who are already in some sense believers. They ask the priest or bishop to confer the sacrament upon them, and we can show them what meaning this sacrament has for the Christian community and can have for them. The couple on the church doorstep asking to arrange a marriage are different. They come in pairs. One may have no Christian commitment at all, the other may have some tenuous family association with this particular local church. We are taught that they each confer this sacrament upon the other, priest and people acting merely as witnesses. Often they are not even aware that they are asking for a sacrament, with all the depth of meaning this has for us of a sacred sign showing forth the work and presence of God. They just want to get married. Obviously the parish community becomes more tentative in suggesting that they prepare for the sacrament of marriage with the seriousness which we think it deserves.

LIMITED INFLUENCE OF MARRIAGE PREPARATION

A way out may be to concentrate in our marriage preparation on the everyday aspects of married life, on such matters as housing and money and 'give and take'. Even here it would be unrealistic to expect spectacular results. The churches are tending to fly to marriage preparation as the great panacea for divorce and marital unhappiness. It is forgotten that the whole of their life experience from birth has slowly prepared this couple for their marriage. Childhood, family, school, friends, work, the adult world: all have shaped their abilities and attitudes. Their influence upon each other is likely to be strong. Beside all this surely a few hours spent with previously unknown parish workers are not likely to change much? Equally, when problems and difficulties arise in the months or years to come, it is extremely unlikely that the couple will either remember what was said during their marriage preparation or have the motivation to put it into practice. This frees parishioners from fears of doing great damage to a couple, but at the same time warns them that to expect marriage preparation alone to stem the flood of marriage breakdown and divorce is just not realistic.

A PARISH TEAM APPROACH TO MARRIAGE PREPARATION

So the parish community, clergy and laity, are left with a puzzle to solve. Every year couples come asking to celebrate their wedding in their midst. The couples are embarking on a risky enterprise and the parish community wants to help all they can. They must offer something relevant, that the couple sees as useful. They must offer something that the couple is ready to receive, that does not presuppose some prior religious conviction which the couple may not hold. They must offer something realistic, that after a few hours' contact will still make some significant contribution to the couple's well-being. And they must do all this in the name of Jesus Christ, whose people they are, who so loved feasting and celebrating and making weddings go with a swing, that at Cana of Galilee he turned water into wine.

In recent years several Roman Catholic parishes have formed

their own marriage preparation team. They offer couples asking to marry in the local church a programme of preparation which goes a long way to meeting the conditions highlighted in this chapter. A scheme for training these parish marriage teams has been worked out by the Catholic Marriage Advisory Council. Whenever the scheme is presented at ecumenical meetings it causes a great deal of interest. The rest of this book seeks to make this scheme better known in Roman Catholic parishes and to share it with the other Christian churches, in the hope that all will adapt it to suit their own resources and objectives. A modest marriage preparation team in every parish would be a small but significant step towards transforming the honest water of the relationship of couples marrying among Christians into the wine of marriage filled with gladness and joy.

3

A Marriage Team for your Parish

There are many possible motives for starting a parish team which will concern itself with marriage preparation. If these are narrowed down to those which are relevant, realistic and readily received, two motives are outstanding.

YOU'RE WELCOME AMONG US

It is indeed a compliment to us, the people of Jesus, that it is among us that this couple have chosen to celebrate the declaration of their life and love together. They deserve a welcome, not only from the priest or minister who is to preside at their wedding, but also from the laity. We are not content that a couple shall book our church as they might hire the hall for their reception. We believe that our local church is the assembly of ourselves far more than that it is the building where we regularly assemble. So we want to meet a couple who choose to marry among us, to make them feel personally welcome and at home. We want to show an interest in them, to get to know a bit about them, and to convey to them that what is important to them is important to us. The couple may meet bureaucracy, impersonality, alienation elsewhere; it shall not be so with us. The first good reason for having a parish marriage team is to ensure for each couple the best welcome we can give them.

To get married today is to be pressurized. There is the pressure of getting together enough money, so that couples are often working overtime or moonlighting, if they have work, or worrying about eking out their unemployment benefit if they have not. There is the pressure of finding somewhere suitable to live and of making it habitable and pleasant. There is the pressure of fulfilling the often contradictory expectations of relatives and friends as they get caught up in a crescendo of wedding arrangements where the logistics of wedding dresses, flowers, caterers, cars, wedding lists, travel plans and family diplomacy assume campaign proportions. The parish marriage team offers time out. Time that is for the engaged couple alone. Some three evenings when there is nothing else to do but for the couple to communicate with each other. The second good reason for having a parish marriage team is for them to give engaged couples time simply to value their own relationship.

WHO MAKE GOOD MARRIAGE TEAM MEMBERS?

Married couples are the best people to do this work, just because they are husband and wife. They are another man and woman with whom the engaged couple can test out their ideas of masculine and feminine roles, of male and female viewpoints and attitudes. They provide another relationship between a woman and a man against which the engaged couple can compare and contrast their own ways of relating.

Friendly and outgoing couples have a head start, those who are interested in other people and enjoy meeting them. They may express diffidence at first, but they should not be too frightened by the idea of working with small groups of engaged couples.

Couples married ten years or less should be considered seriously. Younger couples have much to recommend them. They are not of the same generation as the engaged couples' parents and can be seen as more conversant with the conditions faced by couples starting married life today. They are less likely to talk down from a different era or from a lifetime of experience, and they are usually not already over-committed to other parish ministries. They need not be a perfect couple but should be reasonably confident in their own marriage. Older volunteers who remain approachable by the young need not necessarily be ruled out.

Couples need to be flexible in their attitudes. Their own deep convictions may motivate them to work for the marriage team, but they should be able to allow and expect engaged couples to be different from themselves.

Some couples with differing religious beliefs should always be included in any parish marriage team. Both inter-church and inter-faith couples have important experience to offer. So do couples where only one is a church-goer and the other has no particular religious belief. Most couples asking to marry in our churches will have only one partner who is a member of that particular church. Married couples who share this experience can help them a lot.

Couples roughly matching those getting married in social origins and type of work often achieve the best rapport. This often means looking for volunteers beyond the managerial or committee types who are usually the most active in parish affairs.

HOW DOES THE TEAM PREPARE ITSELF?

A parish marriage team will need some training. Volunteers need to agree a common purpose both between themselves and with the clergy, to practise the necessary skills, and to assemble the resources which will ensure successful meetings with the couples getting married. Training achieves other results, too. It provides a common base-line from which team members will work and a common experience during which volunteers come to know and trust each other. It enables parish clergy to get to know the team couples better and to agree on their respective roles in parish marriage preparation.

WHO PROVIDES THE TRAINING?

One initiative for training parish marriage teams was taken in the Roman Catholic community by the Catholic Marriage Advisory Council, and it is their scheme which is outlined in the following chapters. Several Roman Catholic dioceses, notably the Archdiocese of Liverpool, have also seen the value of the parish team approach and have established their own training, and some parishes have independently decided on a parish-based preparation for marriage and have trained themselves with the help of various experts known to them personally.

It is likely that the movement for training parish marriage teams will gather speed rapidly within the Roman Catholic community in the near future. Already a great surge of energy can be felt from those involved in the Rite of the Christian Initiation of Adults. In this scheme adults asking to join today's Catholic community are not so much given 'instruction', as though it were primarily a matter of absorbing and assenting to information poured in by an expert. During their preparation they spend more time than formerly sharing their faith story with ordinary lay members of the parish, who in turn show them something of their own journey towards trust in Christ and commitment within the Roman Catholic community.

In the catechetical movement there is also renewed emphasis on helping ordinary parishioners to prepare candidates for many of the sacraments. Once again it is not expertise or erudition that is stressed so much as lay-people sharing with candidates the faith and trust that is in them. Very soon now we can expect those in the catechetical movement to look at marriage and to apply their insights and resources to this sacrament in its turn. Then we can hope for adequate training of parish marriage teams to take place within the diocesan catechetical or family support structures and for a less patchy standard of marriage preparation for all couples asking to marry in Roman Catholic churches. This book aims to play a part in bringing this about.

In other Christian churches, too, the parish team approach is being increasingly tried. In the Church of England the Dioceses of London and St Albans have well-tried schemes, and so have many individual parishes. In the Free Churches the importance of marriage preparation has long been recognized. Teams often invite marriage guidance and family-life workers to help in their training, and it is hoped that the following account of the training given by the Catholic Marriage Advisory Council (CMAC) will afford plenty of ideas and methods which these workers can find useful or adapt to suit their own situation.

HOW LONG DOES THE TRAINING TAKE?

There is much to be said for training parish marriage teams during one residential weekend. The team is ready to start work sooner. After such a weekend volunteers feel changed, more committed to the work. They have time at mealtimes, over a drink and in the evening to get to know each other and to feel more of a cohesive group. The rest of the parish feels responsible for organizing child-care facilities for them and to pay for their accommodation, and is likely to value them and use them well on their return. Otherwise training can take place on two consecutive Saturdays, or on six weekday evenings.

Obviously this training is minimal. It is just enough to start a parish marriage team working with some confidence, with some idea of useful topics and methods, and with some concept of what is likely to be acceptable and useful to the engaged couples who are the sole reason for the whole enterprise.

4

Deciding What to Offer

People accept their priest's invitation to join the parish's marriage preparation team from a variety of motives. Very common are: 'He seemed to think we could do it', 'We felt it was our duty to help', or, 'We wanted to oblige the parish clergy'. If clergy are convinced of the value of a team to welcome couples who ask to marry in the parish church and if ordinary parishioners are accustomed to being asked to help candidates preparing for the various sacraments, then enthusiastic parish clergy can usually count on support from obliging parishioners whom they ask directly. If clergy study the profile of people suitable for this ministry outlined in the previous chapter they will approach only those who are sufficiently outgoing, young, flexible and in tune with the couples getting married to do this work well.

Usually volunteers have their own good reasons for wanting to help: 'We get so much from our own marriage. We'd like to pass some of our happiness on to others,' said one parish couple. 'We're really distressed about the way so many marriages break down. We'd like to do our bit to help prevent all that suffering,' added another.

Sometimes volunteers' work gives them something to offer: 'I'm used to PR work with a largely young staff. Perhaps some of my skills will come in useful with couples getting married.'

Sometimes it is as a contrast to their daily occupation that people volunteer, saying, 'It'll make a change from being with kids all day to talk with some young adults,' or, 'I spend my life coping with *things*. It will be a holiday to have a couple of hours a week talking with *people*.'

All these motives can encourage worthwhile volunteers. How acceptable will they be to the couples getting married?

'WILL COUPLES MIND COMING TO SEE US?'

Most volunteers worry that couples will resent being asked to meet them. They have some justification. It is not usually part of a couple's expectations to see anyone except the priest or clergyman who will marry them. Talk of preparation, and especially preparation with a parish team, may provoke remarks like, 'We didn't reckon for all this. We just came to fix up a wedding. You do *do* weddings, don't you?'

The best reply goes something like this: 'We love celebrating weddings with couples like yourselves. Your wedding can be as grand or as simple as you wish. And we'd like to know a bit more about what you think is important in your life together, what exactly you are asking us to celebrate with you. We'd like to give you a chance to know what we think marriage is all about, and to learn this from ordinary members of our church and not just from professional church people like me. That's why in this church we ask you to meet the marriage team. It's our way of saying your marriage is important to all of us who come here on a Sunday. This paper explains our approach. Most couples find they enjoy the meetings. I'll be really glad if you'll give it a try. Shall I ask the team leader to get in touch with you?'

The explanatory handout of one parish goes like this:

Dear Friends

St Erconwald's Church is not only the building where you have decided to celebrate your wedding. It is also a community of all sorts of different people who meet here each week to share their faith in Jesus Christ. The people of St Erconwald's take an interest in all the couples who choose to marry among them.

When you get married at St Erconwald's, you can expect to be welcomed and congratulated not only by the Priest, but also by a couple from the Parish Marriage Team. The Marriage Team consists of young people who have been married for just a few years themselves.

The Team Couple are not experts. They will not try to tell you how to be married. They will not expect your marriage to be like theirs. They will not spend their time talking to you about religion. What they are happy to do is, to welcome you to their home and to give you a chance to relax before all your wedding preparations and take a little time to talk together about yourselves and the sort of marriage you want yours to be.

We hope you will visit your Team Couple two or three times before your wedding. They give their time freely, to show what the people of St Erconwald's think is the most important thing about your wedding – YOU YOURSELVES.

Other parishes are able to arrange group meetings for the couple getting married, and the pleasure of meeting other engaged couples is stressed in their handouts.

If parish clergy spend time explaining the ideas behind parish marriage teams, it is usually quite easy to persuade couples to meet the team. Often couples are delighted that young married people are prepared to take them seriously and to spend time with them, and they are glad to leave the wedding logistics aside to think together about their own relationship. Others may be wary, but prepared to give the idea a try as it seems to be part and parcel of choosing to marry in one particular church. A few may start slightly resentfully but usually they finish praising the team and the programme they offer. 'We didn't expect it to be so interesting, or so much fun' is a typical comment. Only rarely does a couple withdraw from the marriage preparation meetings or refuse to attend at all.

Obviously the whole success of a parish marriage team depends on a worthwhile, acceptable and interesting programme. What do volunteers think they have to offer to couples getting married?

AVOIDING GIVING GOOD ADVICE

Most married couples have a few homely truths which mean a lot to them. Sometimes they are in the form of wise sayings, like 'Bear and forbear' or 'Live and let live', or simple rules like 'Never let the sun go down upon your anger' or 'Always say the Lord's Prayer together at the start of each day'. Some married couples set themselves quite specific regulations, like 'We never eat in front of the television, but always turn it off and sit at a table laid with a clean cloth' or 'No matter how busy our day has been we always try to spend ten minutes in dialogue with each other'. Other married couples will have ritual times when they hug or kiss, like before retiring or on leaving or returning to their home. Such practices are undeniably admirable, but what makes them valuable in any particular marriage is that they have grown out of a couple's own experience of life, they have been freely entered into and they suit the couple's individual personalities, attitudes and lifestyle. Volunteers for parish marriage teams need to realize that engaged couples may well develop their own helpful rituals but that these are not readily copied from another couple who possibly live in very different circumstances. Urging them to take on alien customs is unlikely to be successful and telling them how much a particular ritual means to you is likely merely to increase the distance between you and them. Good advice is often given to a bride and groom but it is not often taken.

Volunteers should think even more carefully if they have attitudes like 'Young people today need to be told that marriage is not a bed of roses' or 'We want to impress on them that they can't get out of marriage as soon as it gets difficult'. It is not young people's fault that marriage today is so fragile. Volunteers are not trying to put engaged couples in the wrong but helping them to improve their chances of getting it right.

Another trap for volunteers is the desire to give expert advice. Faced with a young and inexperienced couple on the verge of making decisions about finding somewhere to live, managing money and a home, and at the beginning of a sexual relationship which could lead to parenthood and family responsibilities, married couples may wish to give them a crash course in conveyancing, insurance, budgeting, home economics, anatomy, physiology and family planning. This is especially tempting if, coincidentally, the volunteer may actually have a particular expertise which seems to be relevant.

It is important for volunteers to be clear that it is not the job of the parish marriage team to give specialist advice. They are not chosen for their professional expertise, neither are engaged couples meeting them because they are in that kind of need. Rather the job of parish volunteers is to help people approaching marriage to express their own attitude to money or homemaking, to sexuality or religion, and to listen to their partner's attitude. In this way they will help the couple to clarify the values which they share.

Where a couple share common values they quickly find for themselves the information needed to put their plans into practice. Parish teams can help them by compiling a list of local experts whom engaged couples may choose to consult: this can include such addresses as the Citizens Advice Bureau, the Samaritans, local family planning clinics or natural family planning teachers, Marriage Guidance Councils or CMAC centres, Alcoholics Anonymous or drug dependency clinics. The list should embrace all the local helping agencies whether statutory or voluntary which the parish team knows to be functioning well, together with individuals who are known by the local church community to be willing to give professional advice to young couples as part of their Christian commitment to others. Such a list will remind parish marriage teams that specialist advice is not their own remit.

A further temptation to be resisted is the desire to influence the engaged couples' decisions far into the future. Such matters as child care, family size, discipline in the home, working mothers, responsibility for elderly relatives, the mid-life crisis and retirement are all important in a lifelong marriage. Opportunity should certainly be sought at key stages for Christians to share feelings, opinions and experiences about topics like these. The point at issue here is that they are not usually on an engaged couple's immediate agenda. Parish volunteers and young couples can easily be seduced into discussing such matters, leaving less time to think about the couple's present circumstances, present hopes and fears, and present way of relating. The best guarantee of a couple clearing future hurdles well is for their present relationship to be as strong as possible. Volunteers aim to help them here and now.

POSITIVE HELP FOR COUPLES GETTING MARRIED

'If we don't give advice or specialist help, and we don't use our experience of marriage to warn couples of troubles ahead, what else can we do?' Volunteers use their experience of marriage as a background to all their work with engaged couples, but the focus of this work is the couple themselves. They are accepted as responsible, well-intentioned people whose relationship already has a history, and who are sure enough of each other to declare their love and commitment before their friends and relations and to ask them to celebrate it in a church before God. Their uniqueness deserves to be taken seriously by the parish community. This is especially so in three important areas.

1. Helping couples to clarify their values. The first aim of a parish marriage team is to look at the whole area of values.

What is important to him and to her? Have they expressed this to their partner? Are they each aware of what matters most to the other? What are their shared aims and goals? What weight in their unique relationship will be given to money, family, sexuality, children, work or religion? What situations in their relationship do they accept happily at the moment, and what makes them dig their heels in and brings out all their stubbornness? What are they striving for, sacrificing for, longing for? What frustrates and blocks them in their plans together? A couple who can see clearly what is important to them and where they want to be are quite likely to get there.

2. Helping couples to sort out their roles.   It may once have been true that a couple who agreed to become wife and husband knew clearly what these roles involved. It is certainly not so today. Who earns the money and decides how to spend it? Who takes responsibility for housework, cooking and shopping? Who maintains a car or the household appliances? Nowadays these are all areas for an infinite variety of individual negotiations and decisions. Today's situation is even more complicated: research shows that even where couples think they share domestic responsibilities equally, in practice many devolve upon the wife to an extent which goes unrecognized by the couple themselves. No wonder that experience of the first years of marriage has been called 'the frustration of expectations'. Helping any particular couple towards their own realistic role allocation is serving them well.

3. Helping couples discover why they want to marry in church.   The bride and groom who are committed members of the church where they marry are exceptional. It is far more common for one of them to ask to marry in a church with which they have some tenuous family connection, and for the other, with no particular religious affiliation, to go along with a church wedding through a desire to please. Sometimes a couple will frankly state that they have chosen a church because it makes a good setting for their photographs, others will say that somehow they 'wouldn't feel married' except in a church. An important service the parish marriage team can offer is to help this couple discover what meaning Christian marriage can have for them.

THE CONTENT OF THE MEETINGS

These three important areas will be the subjects of the team's meetings with engaged couples. Most parish marriage teams have found it a good idea to have three such sessions: the first to get to know the engaged couples, to explore their values and to clarify what is important to them; the second to discuss the whole area of the roles of a wife and of a husband; the third to look at the meaning of Christian marriage and the place of religion in the couple's relationship. The exact content of each of these sessions will be given in chapters 8, 9 and 10.

HOW VOLUNTEERS ARE TRAINED

The method of preparing parish couples to offer these three sessions is quite important. They are asked to work through the same exercises as they will later arrange for the engaged couples. They do not pretend to be engaged, but they look at their own interaction, their own way of relating. They find out what the exercises have to tell them about their own partnership, a partnership which extends from the time they first met, through a time of deeper and deeper commitment until their engagement and marriage, and on to the different phases through which their married relationship has passed. They think, too, about their present ways of relating. This is a benefit to parish couples themselves, as these extracts from their letters show: 'We have the feeling the training may well turn out to be one of the milestones in our own married life,' and, 'Thank you for giving us a time to remember and grow from in terms of our own marriage.' Moreover, working through the exercises for themselves gives volunteers a real understanding of the worth which these exercises can hold for engaged couples.

SKILLS FOR PARISH MARRIAGE TEAMS

Before they feel ready to meet engaged couples volunteers often express their own fears and difficulties about the work

'If we don't tell couples how to be married, and we don't expect them to be married in the same way as ourselves, how on earth can we help them find out how *they* should be married?' asked one volunteer. Another remarked, 'We don't mind meeting just one couple but I'm a bit scared of groups. Won't the whole thing get out of hand?

A third volunteer spoke for many, 'I love my church and I feel very deeply about the things it stands for. I agree that couples must make up their own minds about what is right for them, but am I just expected to condone decisions which I think are wrong? How can I do an official job for my church in this parish marriage team and then let couples get away with decisions my church would not approve?'

The next three chapters will be devoted to skills for the team members themselves: how to listen well, how to cope with groups, and how to help others to make moral decisions.

5

How to Listen

It is one thing for volunteers to agree that it is the couple getting married who are important. It is quite another matter to be able to put that couple first. A couple may be shy, diffident, inarticulate, uninvolved, bored or slightly resentful. They may be brash, superficial or arrogant. They may be evenly matched, or one may appear domineering and hectoring, the other submissive and compliant. The volunteer is not there to judge them, but to accept them as they are. A volunteer aims to help a couple to see where their relationship stands at the moment in the hope of helping them to discover how they want it to grow.

COUPLES NEED TO SEE THAT THE VOLUNTEER IS LISTENING

Getting a couple to start talking about themselves and their relationship is an important part of every session. But they will be encouraged to continue only if they feel that the volunteer is really interested in what they have to say. Couples who feel that the volunteer is attending with only half an ear, or is only waiting for them to finish speaking in order to butt in with something different, soon dry up and opt out. The same happens if couples feel they are involved in some inflexible procedure in which nothing they say makes any real difference to the way the procedure unrolls. Conversely, couples who sense that a volunteer *is* giving them full attention will feel approved and valued, will continue to speak and are more likely to speak at some depth.

Listening well is an important skill for parish marriage team volunteers. There are many exercises designed to help people improve their existing ability to listen, and three such exercises are described here. Volunteers in training are often surprised how much and how vividly they learn about listening by carrying out such exercises. Each exercise is done in pairs.

Listening exercise 1

Take turns to listen for three minutes WITHOUT SAYING ANYTHING AT ALL *to your partners telling you about something which made them really happy. Then ask your partners what it was like to be listened to in this way.*

After this exercise volunteers join the trainer and share what they discovered. Often this exercise runs counter to their normal habits, and they make such remarks as:
'It's very difficult.'
'I kept wanting to ask questions.'
'I wanted to swap a similar story in my own life.'
'I felt I wasn't being any help.'
Yet the experience of being listened to without interruption testifies how effective such listening is:
'I really felt they had time for me.'
'I felt they were really interested in what I was saying.'
'At first I found it hard to keep going, but when I realized they still looked interested and didn't interrupt I found words to express what I wanted to say.'
'I didn't need their words. What kept me going was that they looked at me. They sat facing me looking relaxed but alert, and from time to time they gave encouraging nods and noises.'

Listening exercise 2

Take turns to listen for three minutes to your partners telling you about something which made them rather upset. Show by your body and face that you are interested. Remember to hold back and allow them to tell the story in their own way. If they need encouraging, repeat words they use that seem important to their story. When they have finished, summarize their story for them as you understand it. Then share with each other how the experience felt.

When volunteers join the trainer after this second exercise, those taking the listeners' role often feel better about their part:

'Now that I was concentrating on what my body was saying and on the key phrases, it wasn't so difficult not to interrupt or ask questions.'

'I was surprised that just giving back a few words helped the story forward. The speaker said, "It all seemed pointless," and tailed off. I had only to repeat, "It seemed pointless?" with a bit of question in my voice and he was off again, telling his story with renewed energy.'

Volunteers taking the speaker's part experience how even this minimal intervention is still effective in conveying attention and understanding:

'I felt he was listening and interested in what I had to say.'

'It was nice to have my own story given back to me – it made it seem much less silly and more acceptable, and I could see more clearly what had happened to me.'

'It was good to feel that she checked out what I'd said with me, making sure she'd got it right. So often people run away with half of your story and think they know the whole of it.'

'She didn't get my story quite right at first, but letting me see the way she had understood it gave me a chance to tell her exactly how it really was.'

Listening exercise 3

Take turns for the speakers to think of something they feel strongly about and to recount a recent incident which illustrates it. The listeners must respond with the formula, 'YOU FEEL . . . BECAUSE . . .'. For instance, 'YOU FEEL irritated BECAUSE our daughter always squeezes the toothpaste from the middle of the tube,' or 'YOU FEEL despairing BECAUSE your wife simply can't cope with your hyperactive two-year-old.' Then listeners check with the speakers whether they reflected the speakers' feelings accurately.

When they join the trainer after this exercise it is common for volunteers to have discovered that it is quite difficult for listeners to tune into the feelings behind a story. As one volunteer reported: 'She didn't actually mention how she felt about the toothpaste, simply what her daughter did with it. At first I wanted to say, "You feel that people should squeeze toothpaste tubes from the bottom," but I realized that this neatly bypasses the feeling and so bypasses the clue as to why such a mild practice provokes an angry outburst. It was only as she went on with the story that I realized her predominant feeling was irritation rather than gloom or surprise or something quite different.'

Volunteers also discover that it is quite hard to own our feelings: 'I didn't mention how helpless I feel about the way my wife lets our youngster run rings round her. I tried to give a matter-of-fact and rational account of life in our household. When my wife recognized my underlying feelings and gave them back to me they didn't sound anything to be ashamed of. I experienced a wonderful relief. I felt understood at a fundamental level.'

Of course, any exercises are somewhat artificial, and in the end volunteers do best by being themselves and by finding their own style of working. The value of the exercises to parish couples in training is to bring to mind the skills which will help them convey their genuine care for and interest in the engaged

couples they meet. The exercises also serve to help them practise these skills, and so help the skills to come naturally.

BRUSHING UP LISTENING SKILLS

After a real meeting with engaged couples it is useful for volunteers to give their partner some feedback about the quality of
their listening. Was the room arranged to convey sharing and
intimacy? If it was a group meeting in a hall, were the chairs
in straight rows facing a team seated behind a table, or were
they in a circle where all appeared equally important? If it
was in a private home, was the TV turned off and the chairs
rearranged so that people could all see each other? Did the
volunteer sit facing people as they spoke, relaxed but alert,
without nervous mannerisms? What about eye-contact, encouraging nods and noises, holding back the impulse to butt in?
Did the volunteer manage to encourage the speakers by picking
up their key words, and by checking out their story with a short
summary? How many times did the volunteer 'hit the jackpot'
by voicing really clearly the speakers' feelings and the situation
that triggered them?

Feedback between husband and wife in the parish marriage
team will improve their skills of listening and responding. The
engaged couples they meet will feel understood and are more
likely to give them a glimpse into the way their relationship
works. In this way volunteers will help engaged couples to
discover how they want their relationship to grow.

6

Coping with Groups

'LET'S THROW A PARTY!'

In one parish where the clergy share marriage preparation with a team of lay volunteers it was decided to invite back all the couples who had married in the parish church during the previous year. Twenty recently married couples arrived. What, asked the team, did they remember of the marriage preparation? The couples spoke of an improved understanding of each other, a greater willingness to talk about sensitive issues and to reach some agreement. But what *specifically* did they remember? The newly married couples found it hard to say. Why then attend the reunion, asked the team? That was easy: 'We wanted to meet the others in our group and find out what had happened to them,' explained one new husband.

'We were dying to find out if the others had solved their housing problems,' commented one of the wives. Her husband added: 'We've often wondered how the couple with family difficulties managed to cope.'

'We wanted to compare notes with the other couple who came from two different churches, to see whether they go to each other's church on alternate Sundays like we do,' said an inter-church couple.

'Whenever we negotiate about whose turn it is to make the early morning tea, we wonder whether the others have the same hassle,' smiled another husband, winking at his wife.

This has an important lesson for the churches about the hunger for community and the churches' power to create community. More immediately, the lesson for those planning to offer marriage preparation is also clear. Far more than the marriage preparation programme, engaged couples value the chance to meet each other and to compare and contrast their situations. It follows that group meetings should be offered where at all possible.

GROUPWORK IS A TEAM CHOICE

Not all parish marriage teams can arrange to work with groups of engaged couples. Some volunteers have domestic circumstances which make it easier to meet couples in their own home, and there is not really accommodation for more than four people at once. Some parishes have few weddings quite widely spaced, so that it is impractical to gather groups of couples together at any one time. Some engaged people are on shift-work or live abroad, and the couple finds it hard to meet together regularly and fit in with any group meeting: several couples like this can cause a parish marriage team to decide to abandon any groupwork and to meet couples individually instead.

The couple-to-couple format has the advantage of being easy to arrange, it is less formal, and often the greater privacy allows engaged couples to talk more freely of their attitudes, hopes and fears. Unfortunately it is sometimes difficult for volunteers to inspire sufficient trust for an engaged couple to want to confide in them, and unless the volunteers are already very skilled at getting quickly on terms with strangers a sticky and uncomfortable hour may result. This is less inclined to happen in a group situation, where one or two engaged couples are likely to be naturally self-confident and willing to participate, and so will encourage the others. Even if a given couple choose not to play a full part, in a group setting it is still usual for them to benefit from hearing what others have to say.

31

Parish marriage preparation is best conducted in groups not only because engaged couples often prefer it and parish couples find it less embarrassing. Groups give each member the powerful opportunity for learning which comes from discovering the different experiences, feelings and ideas of the group members:

'I didn't know there were so many ways of looking at the different roles of husband and wife.'

'Now that you've all encouraged us to put our housing problem into words, we see much clearer what we ought to do next.'

'We always agree to differ because we're scared of quarrelling, but the rest of you seem to be able to talk about your differences. Some of you even seem to enjoy your rows and to be good friends afterwards.'

These remarks from couples getting married show that the most important agent for learning can be the group itself.

HANDLING A GROUP

Volunteers may recognize that groups are useful but still feel unsure about taking on large numbers. It is suggested that at first two married couples work with no more than six engaged couples. Here are some hints until they find their own style.

1. Agree beforehand what you want the group to work on, and what you hope to achieve.

2. Set a time for the group discussion to begin and end, and stick to it.

3. Start with a few words which will encourage members of the group to want to participate, and show your interest in what is said as the group progresses.

4. Remember that your main task is to enable every member to contribute, not to give your own point of view.

5. When a member makes a contribution show that you value it by some phrase like 'So you're saying that . . .' or 'You think that . . .'. If the leaders do this often enough, other group members will pick up the habit.

6. Don't worry if groups appear to 'go off the point' a bit. Members need to choose their own way of opting in. They also need to deal with their feelings, such as whom they like and dislike, who is most powerful or most angry, or whether the subject matter stirs emotions because of past experiences. As the group nears its end, bring it back to the main topic, and get members to formulate some conclusions.

SPOTTING WHAT'S HAPPENING

Whole books have been written about the dynamics of groups and the mass of theory can be rather daunting. It helps to remember that much of it applies more to ongoing groups which meet frequently over a prolonged period than to *ad hoc* groups like marriage preparation meetings. Here is one way for volunteers to understand activities often seen in groups, and some ideas on how to cope.

Volunteers choose a group leader and discuss for twenty minutes a question with no very clear solution, such as, 'Is it more difficult for couples getting married today than it was for couples twenty five years ago?' Then they discuss the way their group behaved. The topic is not a good one to suggest to engaged couples because it lacks precision, but volunteers in training are likely to find in discussing it that their group exemplified five important activities which often occur in groups.

1. Fight. Certain members get angry and attack the leader or other members. A good leader tries to acknowledge calmly that the member feels strongly and asks the group to consider any valuable point the angry person makes: 'I can see you're really steamed up about this. Does anyone else find that men often expect women to admire them playing in a match and to make them sandwiches, but never to have a sport of their own they'd prefer to spend time on?'

2. Flight. Some members and sometimes the whole group go completely off the task and chat cosily about comfortable things; they flee the task. A good leader does not belittle people, but eases them back again: 'Can we follow up Martin's point about . . .?'

3. Pairing. There is a natural pairing within engaged couples, but some members will also make alliances with others. A good leader makes sure allies understand each other, and then tries to link them with the other members so that nobody is left out: 'You, Jim, seem to want a quiet Christmas and I think you, Peter, feel the festivities could get out of hand if you don't set severe limits. I imagine most of you find that the whole Christmas thing tends to escalate?'.

4. Scapegoating. Often one member or couple will be out on a limb and consistently maintain a point of view at odds with the majority. The group pushes them further out. A good leader tries to prevent the group dumping all their unowned feelings on the scapegoat: 'You obviously feel strongly that women can't be trusted with chequebooks. It's good to have a different viewpoint. At least we can all agree with you that it's often not easy to reach agreement about money.'

5. Silent and voluble members. Members who won't speak or others who hog the discussion both detract from the group. A good leader picks up non-verbal clues from the silent members: 'You're sighing and shaking your head, Amanda. I wonder what you'd like to say about this?' With over-talkers a good leader is firm: 'You're quite clear, Rupert, that every couple should give a tenth of their income to charity. Will you give the others a chance to say what they think?'

GROUPWORK AS PART OF A SESSION

It is not suggested that the whole of a meeting with engaged couples should be given over to group discussion. Chapters 8, 9 and 10 give extensive examples of material on values and roles in marriage and on the meaning of marriage for Christians. This material is straightforward for the team to present and is worked on by each couple individually. Only after a couple has discussed the topic thoroughly between themselves is it suggested that they will also benefit from hearing what other couples have to say.

The opportunity for engaged couples to learn from each other as a group is a further ingredient of effective parish marriage preparation.

7

What is Right for this Couple?

The marriage preparation team in a Roman Catholic parish were discussing the engaged couples they had met during the year. Stimulating, interesting, various, humorous, full of hope; the couples had enriched the lives of the parish volunteers and were obviously remembered with affection.

WHAT IF VOLUNTEERS THINK COUPLES ARE IN THE WRONG?

One question lingered in the minds of several volunteers: 'Ought I to have said something?' The question arose when any engaged couple gave evidence of values which were at odds with that church's viewpoint. What, volunteers asked, were they to say when couples are living together before marriage, when they argue against the church's stand on contraception or abortion, or when they disagree with the deeply-held convictions of the parish volunteers themselves? How should volunteers respond when they realize that a couple seem incorrigibly materialistic, heedless of church teaching or church practice, or oblivious to the values of the gospel? What if a couple do not believe in God? What should be their attitude to couples who seem to be marrying in church for the sake of the building or the photographs or to please a relative but who set at naught the importance which the church has for those who assemble to worship there?

These questions are the more important to volunteers who have been chosen to form a parish marriage team just because they are convinced Christians. Not for them a take-it-or-leave-it attitude. The reason they are doing 'overtime' with engaged couples is precisely because their commitment to their church is more than average.

Questions such as these are shared by Christians other than Roman Catholics. The Church of England has an obligation to marry all who fulfil the legal requirements. This may result in many of the clergy feeling that their role as a Christian minister is undervalued, and the same can be true of lay-people who work with them. The Free Churches find themselves increasingly asked to celebrate second weddings of Christians from churches which will not recognize the possibility of remarriage for divorced persons. This can often feel like being a poor second option because another church is being too 'choosey'.

The Roman Catholic team who raised these questions finally concluded that marriage preparation is neither evangelization nor catechesis. The aim is neither to win church members, nor to preach the gospel, nor to teach the faith, admirable though all these activities are in other contexts. Marriage preparation is a service the parish offers, reaching out to couples who may not be regular church-members but who ask us to celebrate their relationship according to our custom. They should not be asked to pretend to a commitment to our beliefs and practice that may not exist. We should recognize that their commitment is not to us but to each other. Our job is to value, foster and deepen that commitment, and finally to celebrate it fittingly in the most appropriate ceremony we can offer.

PUSHING OUR VALUES OR CHALLENGING THEIRS

It is not advisable for volunteers to use marriage preparation time to ride particular hobby horses of their own. Devotion to pro-life groups or to the charismatic movement, to Christian CND or to prayer groups may all be admirable, but recruiting for them can be divisive or puzzling in a pre-marriage course and can divert energy from its main purpose.

It is not essential for volunteers to correct or question the beliefs or values of an engaged couple just because these are at variance with their own. The very fact that volunteers are working in a church context gives sufficient witness to their Christian convictions without the need to spell these out explicitly.

DEALING WITH QUESTIONS

What if engaged couples ask questions about faith, practice or moral teaching? Volunteers are certainly not called upon to deny their convictions. Perhaps the best plan is to give their Church's teaching briefly or to sketch out their own standpoint if they wish to do so, and then to return to their main job of preparing this couple for their marriage. Genuine enquirers can be referred to the priest or minister, or lay-people can talk with them individually at another time. All the engaged couples will at least have experienced the Christian church as caring, non-coercive and relevant to their present concern of marrying well.

WHEN A COUPLE DISAGREE

Questions of Christian faith, practice or morality are certainly important to marriage preparation when they cause disagreement between a couple themselves. This is where the skill of volunteers is tested. Their task is tricky. They try to prevent the topic from becoming a no-go area for the couple, who are scared to mention it for fear of exposing fundamental disagreement. They try to help the couple discuss it safely and constructively, summarizing their arguments in turn and tuning into their feelings. If they are in a position to do so, volunteers may gently put them right on errors of fact, or at least ask them to check with a relevant authority, like the priest or minister, whether a supposition is accurate. And then the volunteer allows the couple to come to their own decision.

This may square with volunteers' convictions and with the teaching of their church. Or it may not. Part of the pain of marriage preparation is seeing couples make what seem to be the wrong decisions. It is the pain of Christ who loved the rich young man but let him go.

LEARNING TO HELP

This is an exercise to enable volunteers to see what is involved in helping couples to make their own moral decisions.

Read in turn the following statements from one partner of an engaged couple. In each case EITHER *discuss what you would say to help that couple to understand each other better* OR *carry out a 10-minute role-play of such a couple putting their opinions and of a parish couple helping them to understand each other better.*

ANDY: We've decided to use contraceptives at least for the first few years because we think the Catholic Church is wrong about contraception.

PIPPA: I want to have our children baptized in the local church, but Andy says there's no point because I don't go to church any longer.

PETER: I go along with Anne to church on Sundays sometimes, but it's deadly boring and I don't think I'll go once we have got the wedding service over and done with.

MARTHA   Fred's mother is a bit crippled, but I don't think she should come and live with us. What do you think?

MAUREEN: Bill isn't very reliable with money. He's a milkman and I think the way he does his books is going to get him into trouble soon.

AMANDA (on her own with you in the kitchen): You know I've never told Brian I was engaged to Richard three years ago. I don't think I could because he'd be so upset.

After this exercise volunteers join the trainer to discuss what they have discovered. Often they find that it is hard to concentrate on explaining the couple to each other: 'I kept getting carried away by the rights and wrongs of the argument', said one volunteer. Another added, 'I found it hard not to side with one of the couple against the other.' A third made a useful discovery: 'It's a good idea to stop one of them from time to time and say, "Can you say what she feels?" or, "Do you see what he's saying?" '

Volunteers find their skills of summarizing come in useful: 'Once I concentrated on listening really hard and then telling each what I heard the other saying, I stopped wanting to solve the problem for them and started to help them solve it for themselves.'

Even in role-play, tuning in to feelings hits the jackpot: 'Once I got Bill to see how scared Maureen was that he would lose his job if he went on fiddling the money he moved closer to her and put his arm round her. It was only a role-play, but I felt I'd really helped him to understand her point of view. They were on their way to sorting out their problem.' Empowering couples to make their own moral decisions is much more useful to them than telling them how you think they ought to behave.

At Cana in Galilee the wine failed. Volunteers who offer engaged couples the wine of their own convictions are often puzzled to find it failing, ceasing to have potency for another couple. It seems disappointing to turn to something humbler, to the couple's mutual commitment and to the volunteer's desire to help them understand each other. Yet out of his honest water can come a new wine, freshly pressed for this particular couple.

8

What is Important?
(a first session with engaged couples)

It has been stressed that the first aim of parish volunteers is to
welcome couples asking to marry in their local church. It
follows that they will use all their everyday social skills to
introduce themselves, to ask about the couples and their plans
for their future, and to help couples to talk to each other in a
relaxed and easy manner.

Most parish volunteers do not want a rigid programme laid
down for them to follow slavishly. Often, however, they ask
for guidelines and for a way of getting couples to talk to some
purpose. The three model sessions outlined in the next three
chapters are offered in that spirit. It is fully expected that
volunteers will change and adapt them according to their
circumstances and the needs of the couples they meet.

HELPING ENGAGED COUPLES TO TALK ABOUT THEIR VALUES

If volunteers are agreed not to expect couples to be married in
the same way as themselves, they will want to focus on the
engaged couple's own relationship. What do they want out of
their life together? What are their priorities? What kind of
interdependence are they aiming at, and how will that work
out in their everyday decisions? Certainly they love each other,
but how does this charity work out in practice?

It is not always easy for couples to chat to comparative
strangers about their dearest dreams, even when they are aware
of them consciously. Parish marriage teams look to their

41

training for resources to help them get engaged couples to do this.

One of these resources is the quiz, 'What is important to you?' It is reproduced here, together with the kind of instructions given to married parish volunteers in their training.

THE 'WHAT IS IMPORTANT?' EXERCISE

The best way for you to realize the value of any particular exercise is to work through it yourselves. Do not pretend that you are about to marry. Just look at your present married relationship and see whether the exercise helps your understanding and communication. This first exercise (opposite) is a simple one, designed to help couples discuss their values. Take ten minutes or so to complete it on your own. There are no right or wrong answers.

The next step is for each married couple to compare their answers. If on one person's chart the tick and cross for any item are very far apart, you have something to talk about. One partner perceives a marked difference in your attitudes about something. If the tick on one chart is very far from the cross on the other chart for any item, you have again something to talk about. There is a marked difference in the way you see the same behaviour. Take ten minutes or so to compare your charts and use them as the basis for really frank and open communication between you.

After this exercise volunteers join the trainer for a general discussion. The trainer asks the following sort of questions:
How did it go?
Were there any surprises?
Did it help you to home in on those areas where you still have some thinking and negotiating to do?
Did it help to give specific examples rather than vague generalizations?
Were these easier to accept?

42

What is important to you?

Look at the list below and put a tick in the column indicating the importance you attach to what is mentioned.

	Very	Fairly	Not very	Not at all
Being tidy and well-organized				
Good food				
Being punctual				
Reading				
Football				
Going out regularly				
My own friends				
Family ties				
Inviting people home				
Having time to myself				
Showing affection				
Saying 'I love you'				
Talking together regularly				
Keeping the peace				
Getting my own way				
Honesty				
Keeping promises				
Going to church				
Keeping to a strict budget				
Buying surprise presents				
Saving				
Making careful decisions				
My job				
Promotion				
Living in this area				

Now mark with a cross where you think your partner stands. Try to think of particular conversations or incidents which are influencing your opinions.

Do you see how such an exercise might be helpful to couples getting married?

Do you think you could give engaged people a quiz like this to complete on their own?

Could you encourage each couple to compare charts and to discuss their findings privately?

Could you call couples into a large circle and encourage them to share some of their discoveries?

Would you like to alter the wording of the chart in any way?

THE 'YOUR SORT OF MARRIAGE' EXERCISE

Parish couples will understand from the 'What is important?' exercise that the quiz is not really significant in itself. It is just a trigger for thought, for communication between couples, and for general discussion. When they actually work with engaged couples the group discussion sometimes flows so well after this exercise that it fills the remainder of their first session. Otherwise a second exercise can be used.

Parish couples in training use this exercise in the same way as before: it is completed individually, talked over by couples on their own, then made the subject of general discussion.

Your sort of marriage

1. Do you want your marriage to be like your parents' marriage?
2. Are his/her parents very different from yours? In what way?
3. Are you like either of yours? Is he/she like either of his/ hers?
4. What was the attitude in your family towards nudity and sex?
5. Do you like to express your love by gesture, touch, in front of others?

6. Do you like your partner to do this?
7. What part does religion play in your relationship and do you talk about it or consciously avoid it? If so, why?
8. What are your views about drink?
9. How will you celebrate next Christmas?
10. Does your partner think that rows are a good thing to clear the air?
11. How does your partner make it up after a disagreement?
12. Does your partner think that marriage is until death?
13. 'Something that scares me about being married is . . .'
14. 'I'd like my partner to understand that I get worked up about . . .'

When parish volunteers actually come to work with engaged couples they may find that there is not time to use this exercise. In this case they can suggest that engaged couples take it home and work on it by themselves. Couples often continue the discussion in the time between sessions, and this can be encouraged. Often they seem transformed at the start of the next session, bubbling over with tales of their discussions and debates which have taken place in the meantime. Asking about this is a good way for parish volunteers to start the second session.

9

Who Does What?
(a second session with engaged couples)

'We don't want to be a husband or a wife, we just want to get married.' This remark from a young man sounded rather obscure, but his girl-friend nodded eagerly.

'We want to be together, to live our lives together,' she said. 'What we don't want is for other people to tell either of us to do this or that just because we're married.' This couple were expressing the wish to negotiate their roles between themselves, not to have them ascribed by custom or culture.

DOMESTIC ROLES NEED TO BE NEGOTIATED

It is certainly true that the roles of husband and wife appear much more open to negotiation than in former times, but this may be misleading. Research shows that new and childless husbands and wives often think they share domestic tasks equally, whereas investigation reveals the major responsibility devolves far more heavily on the wife. Some couples will insist that they carry an equal share when the only household task a husband actually carries out regularly is to put out the rubbish, and his wife bears the major responsibility for shopping, cooking, cleaning and other chores. In such cases the expectation of a life of equal sharing is likely to meet with frustration and disillusion as the true state of affairs gradually dawns.

Apart from social trends, couples have personal preferences about the division of labour in the home, and individual skills which may make it more advisable for one to carry out certain tasks rather than the other. They also have different role models from their own parents, which they may want to copy or to contradict, or on which they may base assumptions about role behaviour which they never voice but which underlie their judgement of their partner's performance.

'I like French cooking,' one young man explained, 'so I make the *coq au vin* while she does the wallpapering.' 'It's better that way,' his girl agreed. 'He can't match the patterns to save his life, and scrambled egg is about my limit.' 'I used to think she was a pretty poor sort of wife,' said one young husband. 'She never even got me a morning cup of tea. We were six months married before I discovered that she was thinking just the same about me. It took us that long to realize that in her family her father always got the early morning tea, and in mine it was my mother. After that we took it in turns. And we appreciated the times we were given tea instead of taking it for granted.'

ATTITUDES TO WORK NEED TO BE NEGOTIATED

Another sphere which requires negotiation is a couple's working life. The new husband and wife find themselves in an age which pays lip-service to equality in the workplace but where women often find themselves at a disadvantage. How will this affect a couple's job decisions? What impact does actual or threatened unemployment have on a couple's ability to set up a home? What relation do job decisions have to the decisions about postponing or starting a family? How do a couple's parents affect their assumptions about the roles of husband and wife at work? How do they each evaluate the importance of paid work compared with work in the home, and how does this affect the respect they have for each other and their own self-esteem?

47

Roles at home and at work

Put a tick if you agree with the statement.

Put a cross if you disagree.

Then compare your choices with your partner and try to say why you think as you do.

I would like us to divide up the household tasks in much the same way as my parents did.

Some jobs in the house are really women's work. (If so, which?)

It is important to work out clearly which household jobs are the husband's responsibility and which are the wife's.

If a household job needs doing, both husband and wife should always be equally prepared to do it.

Wives should look for less tiring paid work than their husbands because they will be more responsible for running the home.

Husbands have to put more energy into their paid work than wives into theirs.

If my partner is out of work I will still regard him/her in the same way.

If I am out of work I will still value myself as much as I do now.

This is a good trigger for discussion. Married volunteers use it in their training to explore their own attitudes first alone, then as couples and finally as a team. It is then recommended that when they work with engaged couples the quiz is used in the same three-stage fashion. It has proved valuable in helping couples to talk not merely about their domestic and working decisions, but also about their underlying attitudes.

THE ROLES OF HUSBAND AND WIFE ARE ALSO SEXUAL

It would be unrealistic to discuss the roles of husband and wife without recognizing that marriage is a sexual relationship. Founded on sexual attraction, enriched by sexual intimacy, their unity is symbolized, nourished and expressed by full sexual intercourse.

Christians believe sexuality is good and God-given. Husband and wife who please each other in sexual intercourse are also pleasing to God. In loving sexual intercourse the body is redeemed, and self is communicated to the partner.

The reality does not always live up to the ideal. Whether or not there has been pre-marital intercourse, sexual adjustment is not automatic. There are skills to be learned, and more importantly there is another person to be learned, considered and pleasured. The shared sexual experience needs to be reflected upon together so that it comes to symbolize for both partners their shared life and love. One gift married volunteers can give to engaged couples asking to marry in their local church is to help them enter marriage able to put into words their feelings about their married sexual relationship.

If a couple can find the words they can more readily seek sexual information or counselling in the few cases where this is necessary. Much more importantly they can help each other to express their love skilfully and can reflect together upon

49

their sexual life so that it comes to express the whole relationship which they share.

THE JEFF AND LIZ EXERCISE

Putting sexual experience into words is not easy; words can seem too medical, too crude, too colloquial, too coy, too elevated or too removed from everyday life. This exercise uses everyday expressions which have proved readily understood by married and engaged couples. The exercise is built around a couple who have been married for a short while, to avoid having to distinguish engaged couples with experience of sexual intercourse from those who are still virgins. Putting the exercise at one remove from personal experience also makes couples feel safer in risking discussion of such an intimate topic. Married couples in training help their partner to talk about the attitudes expressed and share their feelings about them. Then the team joins the trainer for an open discussion about the sexual matters raised. Each team finishes by considering whether they feel comfortable with the wording and would feel happy to use this exercise with engaged couples. They are, of course, free to re-write it as they wish. Sexuality being such a personal and sensitive issue, it is not surprising that this quiz is rewritten more often and more variously than any other.

It is not easy today for married couples to see clearly the domestic, work or sexual roles which they wish to assume. Neither is it easy for wife and husband to harmonize their roles, so that their relationship runs smoothly in a way that is mutually satisfying. They will need to negotiate honestly and often to realize harmony; to gain mutual satisfaction they will need to sustain each other, heal each other and help each other grow. Here we touch upon the meaning that marriage can have for Christians.

Sexual roles

Jeff and Liz have been married for nearly a year. These are some of the things they have said to each other about sex during that time.

Try telling your partner whether or not you think each statement is justified, and why.

Jeff has told Liz:

Just because I still like looking at girlie magazines, it doesn't mean I don't love you.

It would turn me on a lot better if you wore more sexy underwear.

I wish you wouldn't always expect me to make the first move. Why can't *you* suggest having sex sometimes?

I want to satisfy you but I'm not sure how. Will you show me what turns you on?

I want to tell you what I'd really like us to do when we have sex, but I'm afraid you'd either be shocked or laugh at me.

I love having sex with you and helping you enjoy it too. When I think that God made sex for us to enjoy each other like this, it changes my whole idea of God.

Liz has told Jeff:

It bothers me that other pretty girls can still get you going. Can't you realize you're married to me now?

Why can't we just kiss and cuddle sometimes? Why do you always have to go all the way?

I wish you'd realize that I have to get in the mood before I'm ready to have sex.

When we have sex, will you sometimes tell me in words how it feels to you?

When I'm lit up after we have sex, why do you always turn over and go to sleep and leave me up in the air?

Sex with you makes me feel right and reminds me who I belong with. I'm beginning to see how God gave us sex to help us become one.

Perhaps you might try sometime soon to tell your partner something you think about sex but haven't got round to saying before now.

10

What Can Marriage Mean for Christians?
(a third session with engaged couples)

Those Christians who say that marriage is a sacrament know that this is about naming everyday experience, pointing to its transcendent significance and celebrating the presence of God within the everyday event. Christians from other traditions which do not cite marriage as one of the sacraments still want to do something very similar: to pause in the rush of wedding preparations, to reflect upon the meaning of a woman and a man choosing each other as life partners, and to celebrate the event before God with joy and gladness.

If an engaged couple chooses to marry in a Christian church they are entitled to know what their wedding signifies to the Christian community. Parish marriage teams are usually chosen from Christians more than averagely committed to their church. This can give rise to a situation where the parish couple use churchy language to paint a religious picture which has no meaning for the engaged couple before them and does not seem to touch their daily life and experience. The result is a monologue or sermon on one side, blank looks or uneasy shuffling on the other. Usually the engaged couple preserve an air of polite attention but there is no honest meeting of minds. Parish volunteers feel this and are reluctant to repeat the experience.

The three exercises which follow give volunteers in training an opportunity to understand the meaning of Christian marriage in a way which is equally valid for believers and for unbelievers and which prevents religion from becoming a no-go area between them. During their training volunteers apply these exercises to their personal history as married couples. Later they ask engaged couples to look at the shorter history of their particular relationship, from the time they first met until they came together to ask for a wedding in a Christian church.

THE 'SPECIAL MOMENTS' EXERCISE

Spend ten minutes as a couple thinking of times since you met which were really important to both of you. Important to your shared history. Special times. Significant. Turning points. Moments not to be forgotten. Remind each other about how it was.

This is a satisfying exercise for volunteers who, after the ten minutes, seem to glow as they return for discussion with the trainer. Some do not want to share their memories and need not be forced to do so. Others speak of them freely: the time they moved into their first home, and sat on packing cases to eat their sandwiches: the time a husband drove through the night with his wife and children sleeping in the car, and he thought 'All I love is here, entrusted to me'; the time a couple climbed a lonely hill and a golden eagle rose into the air, hovering before them; the time a child was in danger of death, and they coped together.

One volunteer pulled a tattered, dog-eared note from his wallet. It said 'Dear Steve. Thank you for fixing my car. Love, Jackie.' It represented a quarrel when they were engaged to be married. He could not think how to make it up, so mended her old banger instead. Her brief letter re-established communication between them and showed him all was well again. 'I've always kept that note,' he said simply.

When Christians want to talk about what is important or significant, they use the word 'God'. Believers can say God or God's love is at work, or present, or with them in all the special moments described. This way of considering where God is in a marriage is often new to parish volunteers, and it provides them with a way of introducing the meaning of Christian marriage to engaged couples which finds a ready response.

THE 'EVERYDAY HELP' EXERCISE

Spend ten minutes as a couple thinking of all the ways you rely on each other every day. What ordinary things do you depend upon each other for? What can you take for granted that your wife or husband will do for you? What everyday help would you miss if your partner went away for a week, or was in hospital for ten days?

Volunteers can usually produce long lists after this exercise. One group of items includes such practical matters as making tea, seeing the store cupboard is stocked, carrying out household repairs, and going in to work whether feeling inclined or not.

A second group of items on the volunteers' lists usually mentions kindness from one partner to the other:
'He always calms me down!'
'She'll listen to me telling the story of the day's events.'
'He hears my worries and troubles.'
'She always has time for me, where my own mother never never seemed to.'
'He's somebody who knows and cares whether I live or die.'
'Just being a father and a mother makes us much surer of our sexual identity – we've got each other to thank for that.'

A third group of items commonly listed by volunteers includes ways a husband and wife may have of encouraging each other:
'She expects me to attend the kids' school functions, and I won't let her down.'
'He thinks I can decorate the house well, and I find myself getting better and better at it.'

'He's always encouraged me to work outside the home and made it possible for me to do so.'

'She takes pleasure in my success at work, even though it means we have less time together.'

After volunteers have listed all the ways in which they experience helpfulness between husband and wife, the trainer collects their items on a flipchart in three such groupings: the practical help, the kindnesses and the encouragement. Volunteers are then reminded of Dr Jack Dominian's assertion that people today marry in order to sustain each other, to heal each other and to help each other to grow. What is this practical help, if not husband and wife sustaining each other? What is this kindness, if not healing the wounds inflicted by the past or by the outside world? What is this encouragement, if not husband and wife helping each other to grow and develop their own strengths? Volunteers can readily see that their own married relationships exemplify the sustaining, healing and growth promotion which Dr Dominian tells us are the main reasons today for marrying and staying married.

Christians can go further. Wherever there is sustaining, Christians see the activity of God the Father, creator and sustainer of all. Wherever there is healing, Christians see the presence of God the Son, redeemer and healer. Wherever there is growth, there Christians see the work of God's life-giving Spirit. In the everyday examples of sustaining, healing and helping growth which are experienced in ordinary marriages, Christians can point to the presence of the Trinity, the presence of God. This way of discovering God at work in their marriage gives new meaning for volunteers to St John's 'Where love is, there is God'. They are then able to introduce this to engaged couples in a way that finds an echo in the hearts of believers and nonbelievers alike.

THE PINCH-CRUNCH FLOW-CHART

This last exercise is adapted from an idea of Sherwood, who uses a flow-chart to explain how a relationship works and what happens when it goes wrong. Here the flow-chart is used to look at the relationship of a couple asking to marry. It begins with their meeting and looks at the interaction which has brought them to their present stage of commitment, and looks at their continuing interaction after their marriage. Couples training to work in a parish marriage team often say that this flow-chart gives them insight into the way their own marriage is working. It also provides them with a useful means of showing an engaged couple how the marriage relationship starts, develops and changes.

The marriage relationship can be described by the following consecutive steps:

1.

A couple from different backgrounds and with different personalities meet. Each has a suitcase full of abilities to bring, each has a jumble-bag full of unsorted past experiences and emotions to conceal.

2.

Sharing information
Negotiating expectations

They find out something about each other. They discover what kind of behaviour the other takes for granted. They see whether their assumptions are congruent.

3.

Clarifying roles
Commitment

If they wish, the couple may now decide to enter into some kind of relationship. They work out what they may expect of each other and what each is willing to do for the other. They undertake to fulfil these expectations. They have a common purpose.

4.

'STABILITY'

If they wish, the couple may now enter into a period where they actually fulfil the other's expectations. Everything about the relationship seems fine.

5.

PINCH
choice point
(experienced by one)

Inevitably and inexorably, periods of stability are followed by a PINCH. This is where one partner feels unhappy, annoyed, depressed, or feels some other strong emotion which shows forcibly that something is going awry in the relationship. The other partner cannot see what all the fuss is about.

6.   Three outcomes are possible. The person feeling the pinch may ignore it, and pretend everything is still fine. This may restore stability for a time, but inevitably there will be a recurrence of the pinch. The person feeling the pinch may say, 'I'm not happy. It's not working, is it?' and the couple will settle down to talk the problem over openly and to find a remedy. Or the person feeling the pinch may not be able to tell the other about the difficulty, but in some roundabout way may manoeuvre so that the problem is renegotiated indirectly. These last two methods carry a risk of breaking the relationship, but some sort of renegotiation is needed if stability is to be restored. The process is illustrated opposite.

An engaged couple will have gone round this cycle many times before they reach the kind of stability which enables them to approach a Christian church to arrange a wedding. A husband and wife will go round this cycle hundreds of times more. Pinches properly negotiated are growing points and their successful resolution makes a relationship stronger.

7. If pinches are ignored, they never go away. The couple enter into a period of increasing unhappiness. 'What on earth are you playing at?' 'What do you want from me?' 'I can't forgive or forget!' 'You're driving me mad!' The couple reach a CRUNCH, where each blames the other and causes the other's unhappiness. For instance, he comes home late because she nags while she nags because he comes home late. Or, she is unfaithful because he drinks while he drinks because she is unfaithful.

8. A crunch has four possible outcomes: (i) Starting again without facing the underlying problem leads eventually to more misery and another crunch. (ii) Unresolved crunches may end

The Marriage Relationship

How it works and when it doesn't

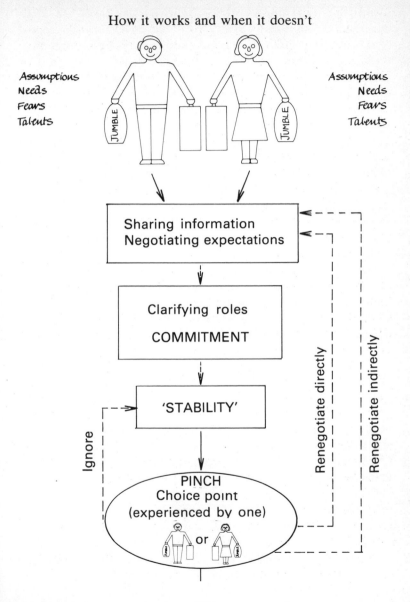

in bitter divorce. (iii) Otherwise couples stay together for security or respectability or for the children's sake, but their marriage is emotionally dead. (iv) The only outcome which saves the relationship is painful, honest and time-consuming renegotiation of the kind that couples find in marriage counselling and which is not often possible without skilled help. The full PINCH-CRUNCH flow-chart is shown opposite.

The PINCH-CRUNCH flow-chart can help volunteers to see that where pinches are inevitable, crunches are not. They can be avoided by proper negotiation of pinches. Married couples are not helpless victims of marital fragility today, they can do something to help themselves.

Every healthy marriage has pinches. The proper Christian response to a pinch is not to ignore it, put up with it or 'offer it up'. There is a place in marriage for stoicism and self-sacrifice but this becomes distorted when partners too often attempt unilateral solutions to their problems.

Marriage involves a mutuality, a commitment to face life and to solve life's problems together. Much harder and much riskier than bearing troubles bravely, the proper response for married Christians is to admit that something is wrong and to ask their partners for help in solving the difficulty. Negotiation of pinches takes time and can be tedious, but it is necessary so that crunches can be avoided. This is true reconciliation, the metanoia or conversion to which all Christians are called. True married spirituality is for the wife and husband to show the love which time and time again acknowledges that there is a problem, negotiates a solution and so seeks for true reconciliation.

Volunteers sometimes puzzle about the difference between Christian marriage and good, human marriage. I believe deeply that God is at work in all marriages, in the peak experiences, in the daily cherishing, in the continual reconciliation. Who can set limits to God's activity? Christians have the privilege of reflecting on this presence, of recognizing God in their marriage and pointing God out to each other, naming God by name. And over a lifetime I believe this naming changes the quality of a marriage, in an indefinable way enriching it.

The Marriage Relationship
How it works and when it doesn't

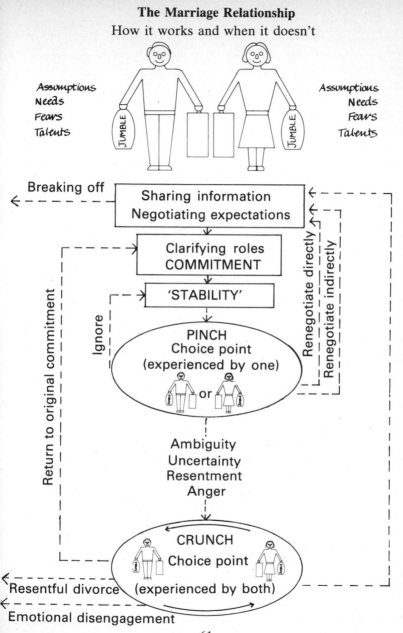

At most weddings there is wine: wife and husband bring joy to each other and are glad. But Christians believe that the best wine for a wedding, the greatest gladness, comes through the transforming power of Jesus Christ. Not every couple recognizes this source of their joy, just as the steward at Cana did not know the source of the improved wine. Yet the steward had no doubt about its quality. To those who know Jesus Christ, to his disciples, he lets his glory be seen, and two-by-two they recognize him in their married love. And they believe in him.

MARRIAGE is —
knowing GOD through the
deep experiences shared by
a man and a woman

MARRIAGE is —
experiencing GOD
as Father, Son and Spirit
when husband and wife
sustain each other,
heal each other and
help each other to grow

MARRIAGE is —
a permanent commitment
to a reconciling love.

Ten Hints for Parish Marriage Teams

1. Work *with* your parish clergy. It is their job to see that couples are ready for marriage; your job is to help them.

2. Don't give couples specialist advice. Compile a list of local agencies that could help them, such as Legal Aid, Citizens' Advice Bureau, Marriage Guidance Council or Catholic Marriage Advisory Council centre, family-planning clinic or natural family-planning teacher, local housing department or housing association.

3. Aims of parish marriage teams: to welcome couples asking to marry in your local church; to help them talk together about their hopes and problems; to help them resolve 'pinches' so that their relationship lasts; to help them see their marriage as a sign of God's presence.

4. Couples may not want to see you at first. Your job is to welcome them and work with them in such a way that they benefit from seeing you and even enjoy it.

5. Each couple is different. Try to listen to them. Don't expect them to be like yourselves.

6. Share a little of your own experience if it helps to start the couple talking more freely. Let them see you as 'a marriage in action'; do not pretend to be an ideal couple.

7. Do not think you must become an official spokesman for the Christian church. Be honest in what you say, to your conscience and to your understanding of Christianity.

8. A good way of working with couples is to ask them to complete a quiz individually, then to discuss it with their partner. After that they will probably be ready to share a general discussion with you and with other couples. Useful exercises are:

What is important to you?
Your sort of marriage
Roles at home and at work
Sexual roles
Special moments as a sign of God's presence
Daily married life as a sign of God's presence.

9. Explain the PINCH-CRUNCH flow-chart to engaged couples. Help them to see that PINCHES are inevitable in a healthy marriage, but CRUNCHES can be avoided by honest and open negotiation. Show that Christian marriage involves daily commitment to a reconciling love.

10. Enjoy this work, and the couples will enjoy it too.

Notes and References

page 3: *Lumen Gentium*, art. 31 and art. 33.

page 5: 1983. Source: Office of Population, Censuses and Surveys. The 1984 figures released recently show that 69% of people marrying for the first time did so in church.

pages 13–14: The scope of these changes can be assessed from the following books:

The Rite of Christian Initiation of Adults (Centre for Parish Catechetics, 23 Kensington Square, London W8 5HN).

Our Faith Story, A. Patrick Purnell (Collins).

We Celebrate the Eucharist, Christiane Brusselmans (Silver Burdett).

Living the Faith Together, Wim Saris (Collins).

page 14: *Preparation for Marriage*, St Albans Diocesan Family Life Education Project (41 Holywell Hill, St Albans, Herts).

page 26: Some of the best training exercises in interpersonal skills are described in *You and Me*, Gerard Egan (Brooks/Cole Publishing Co). It is well worth translating the American jargon to get to the valuable core.

page 33: Two non-frightening books about groupwork are *The Red Book of Groups*, Gaie Houston (The Rochester Foundation, 8 Rochester Terrace, London NW1) and *Once upon a Group*, Michael Kindred (Southwell Diocesan Education Committee, Dunham House, Westgate, Southwell, Notts, NG25 OJL).

page 46: *Young People and Marriage*, Penny Mansfield (Scottish Marriage Guidance Council).

page 49: *Embodiment*, James B. Nelson (Augsberg, Minnesota).

page 52: *Sacramental Basics*, Tad Guzie (Paulist Press).

page 55: *Marriage, Faith and Love*, Jack Dominian (Darton, Longman & Todd).

page 55: This flow-chart is based on the Pinch and Crunch model of planned renegotiation developed in America by Sherwood and Glidewell.

Some Useful Addresses

ASSOCIATION OF INTER-CHURCH FAMILIES
The Old Bakery, Danehill, Haywards Heath, Sussex RH17 7ET.
    A resource for all concerned with marriages between committed Christians of different church allegiances.

BRITISH COUNCIL OF CHURCHES DIVISION OF COMMUNITY AFFAIRS
2 Eaton Gate, London SW1W 9BL
    Publishes 'Preparing for Marriage', a folder for ministers and clergy offering marriage preparation.

CATHOLIC MARRIAGE ADVISORY COUNCIL
15 Lansdowne Road, London W11 3AJ.
    Counsellors at 70 centres throughout England and Wales run pre-marriage courses and train parish pre-marriage teams, as well as counsel individuals and couples.
    Publishes a booklet 'Your Future Begins Now' for pre-marriage counsellors.

CHURCH PASTORAL AID SOCIETY
Falcon Court, 32 Fleet Street, London EC4.
    Publishes 'Side by Side' a marriage preparation kit containing videos, quizzes and discussion sheets.

HOUSE OF BISHOPS MARRIAGE EDUCATION PANEL
Church House, Deans Yard, London SW1P 3NZ.
    A focus for the concern of the Church of England for marriage preparation. Publishes a booklet 'Preparing Couples for their Wedding'.

Herbert Gray College, Littlechurch Street, Rugby, Warwickshire CV20 3AP.

In addition to its remedial counselling service NMGC provides an education service, and local councils in some places run marriage preparation courses. Publishes a booklet for couples, *Preparing to Marry*.

Walton Hall, Milton Keynes, MK7 6AA.

Programmes for education in relationships.

75 Station Road, West Horndon, Brentwood, Essex.

In addition to structured weekends for married couples this movement also offers weekends known as Engaged Encounter for couples about to marry.